بِسْمِ اللهِ الرَّحْمٰنِ الرَّحِيْمِ

In the Name of Allah, the Most Gracious, the Most Merciful

This book is a special gift
to a special child from Allah

May it bring you closer to His love, mercy, and light

What Islam Teaches Me

Introducing Islam to Your Muslim Offspring

The Sincere Seeker Collection

Riiiing! goes the school bell.

"Bismillah!" I say.
I close my locker.

I run, run, run to class —
my backpack bouncing behind me.

I don't want to miss today's lesson!
Oh—by the way,
my name is Rashad!

Hurry! I'll meet you in class!

"Assalamu Alaikum, little ones!"
Teacher Amal smiles.
"Come sit on the colorful carpet."

I sit crisscross on the soft floor.
My eyes grow wide.

"Today," she says,
"we will learn about Islam —
the beautiful way Allah
wants us to live!"

"Ooh! I love adventures!" I whisper.

Teacher Amal asks,
"Who knows our Creator's name —
the One who made the sky
and the land?"

My hand shoots up.
"Ooh! Ooh! I know!"

"Yes, Rashad?"
"Allah!" I say with joy.

"Alhamdulillah! Perfect,"
says Teacher Amal.

Tap, tap, tap!
We hear a sound.

At the window is a tiny bluebird.
Peck, peck! goes his little beak.
He tilts his head.
He looks at us.

"Oh my!" says Teacher Amal.
She opens the window.
The little bird hops closer.
He looks hungry.

"What should we do," asks Teacher Amal,
"when someone needs help?"
"Help them!" we all say together.

Teacher Amal reaches into her desk.

She takes out a small bag of juicy red berries.

She places the berries gently on the sill.

"In Islam, we are kind to all of Allah's creatures," she says with a smile.

The little bluebird pecks happily. "Tweet, tweet!"

It sounds like he's saying, "Thank you!"

Teacher Amal turns back to us.

"Now, little stars...
Who knows the name of Allah's
special Book that holds
all His beautiful Words?"

Hands shoot up everywhere —
"The Quran!" we all shout together.

"Yes! Perfect!"
she says with a big smile.

"But remember... gentle voices,
and raise your hand before speaking."

Knock, knock!
goes the classroom door.

"Come in!" calls Teacher Amal.

Principal Zoya steps inside
with a shy boy by her side.

"Assalamu Alaikum, everyone!"
she says warmly.

"This is Jamal, our new friend.
He just moved to our town!"

"Wa Alaikum Assalam, Jamal!"
we all reply.

"Welcome!" I wave happily.
I can't wait to be his friend!

After Jamal finds his seat,
Teacher Amal asks,
"What do we call someone who
believes in Allah ﷻ and tries their very
best to follow His loving rules?"

My classmate Malika
raises her hand politely.
"A Muslim!" she says confidently.

"That's correct, Malika!"
Teacher Amal smiles warmly.
"Well done!"

I grin and whisper to myself,
"That's me!"

"Here's a special question,"
Teacher Amal says with a smile.

"Can anyone name the special messenger
Allah ﷻ sent to teach us about Allah,
how to live, and be our best selves?"

I notice my friend Kareem looking down.
His hand starts to go up,
then drops again.

He looks a little shy.
Kareem glances at me and whispers,
"I'm scared to answer."

I lean closer and whisper,
"You can do it, Kareem!"
I give him an encouraging smile.

Kareem takes a deep breath, sits up tall, and raises his hand high.

"Yes, Kareem!"
Teacher Amal encourages.

"Is it... Prophet Muhammad ﷺ?"
he asks with a brave smile.

"YES!" Teacher Amal cheers.
"And remember — whenever we say his name, we say 'peace be upon him' to show love and respect."

Kareem lets out a relieved breath.

I give him a gentle nudge to high-five him.

Tap, tap!
Our little bluebird friend is back at the
window —but this time, he looks thirsty.

Teacher Amal smiles and
fills a tiny bowl with cool water,
placing it gently outside.

"Just like Prophet Muhammad ﷺ
taught us," she says,
"we care for all living things."

The bluebird dips his beak into the bowl.

Sip... sip... sip.

"Prophet Muhammad ﷺ taught us many wise and beautiful things," Teacher Amal explains as we watch our feathered friend drink.

"His sayings are called Hadith, and when we follow his way, it's called the Sunnah."

"Like being kind to animals?" asks Jamal, our new classmate.

"Exactly like that!" Teacher Amal smiles.

"Chirp-chirp!" sings the bluebird, as if thanking Teacher Amal — then he flutters away happily.

Teacher Amal smiles.
"Big question time!" she says.
"Why did Allah ﷻ create us?"

The room goes super quiet.
We think and think.

"It's okay, little ones,"
Teacher Amal says gently.

"Allah ﷻ made us to worship Him.
We worship Him by loving Him,
praying, and being kind."

"Muslims believe in six things,"
says Teacher Amal,
counting on her fingers:

- One Allah ﷻ — our Creator.
- His angels.
- His messengers.
- His books, like the Quran.
- The Day of Judgment.
- Allah's perfect plan — called al-Qadr.

"These are our beliefs," she explains.
"We keep them safe in our hearts."

"Islam also has five special pillars,"
says Teacher Amal,
showing us a colorful chart:
• Shahada — believe in Allah and His
messenger Muhammad ﷺ.
• Salah — pray five times a day.
• Zakat — give to people in need.
• Sawm — fast in Ramadan.
• Hajj — visit Makkah if we can.
"These are our actions," she smiles.
"They help us grow strong in faith."

Shahada — believe in Allah and His messenger. ﷺ

Salah — pray five times a day.

Zakat — give to people in need.

Sawm — fast in Ramadan

Hajj — visit Makkah if we can.

"One last question," says Teacher Amal.
"What is the reward for believing and doing good?"
"Jannah! Paradise!" we shout.
"Yes!" says Teacher Amal.
"Jannah is our happy home with Allah forever — full of joy and peace!"

Riiiing! The bell rings.
We pack our bags.
Teacher Amal brings out a shiny gold foil bag.
Inside are little delicious choco-lates!
Beeeeep! goes my dad's car horn.
I see him through the window, waving with a big smile!
I grab my backpack and wave goodbye to all my friends.

I hop in the car.
"How was school?" Dad asks.
"It was amazing!" I say.
"We learned about Allah.
We helped a bluebird.
We made a new friend.
We learned our beliefs and pillars.
And we even got a treat!"
"Alhamdulillah," says Dad.
"I'm proud of you."

The End

May this journey bring you closer to
Allah's ﷻ infinite love and wisdom.

www.ingramcontent.com/pod-product-compliance
Lightning Source LLC
Chambersburg PA
CBRC090840120626
46551CB00008B/709